PENGUIN TWENTIETH-CENTURY CLASSICS

SELECTED POEMS: FERNANDO PESSOA

Fernando Pessoa was born in Lisbon in 1888 and was brought up in Durban, South Africa. He matriculated at the University of Cape Town, where he won the Queen Victoria Prize for English Essay. In 1905 he returned to Lisbon where he matriculated at the University, and continued to read and write in English. He published in 1918 *35 Sonnets* and in 1922 the three parts of his *English Poems*, all composed many years before. The rest of his life passed uneventfully in Lisbon. He earned a pittance from a number of commercial firms, composing free-verse and classical odes in the intervals of translating the firm's foreign correspondence. Some of his poems were published in literary journals. Pessoa also wrote prose on questions of aesthetics, and sketches for detective novels. The only book published in his lifetime was *Mensagem*, a collection of poems on patriotic themes which won a consolation prize in a national competition. Pessoa also wrote under three pseudonyms, Alberto Caeiro, Alvaro de Campos and Ricardo Reis, whose biographies he invented. He died in 1935.

Selected Poems

Fernando Pessoa

Translated by Jonathan Griffin

Second edition
with new Supplement

 Penguin Books

PENGUIN BOOKS

Published by the Penguin Group
Penguin Books Ltd, 27 Wrights Lane, London w8 5tz, England
Penguin Putnam Inc., 375 Hudson Street, New York, New York 10014, USA
Penguin Books Australia Ltd, Ringwood, Victoria, Australia
Penguin Books Canada Ltd, 10 Alcorn Avenue, Toronto, Ontario, Canada m4v 3b2
Penguin Books (NZ) Ltd, Private Bag 102902, NSMC Auckland, New Zealand

Penguin Books Ltd, Registered Offices: Harmondsworth, Middlesex, England

This section first published by Penguin Books 1974
Second edition with new Supplement published 1982
10 9 8 7 6 5 4

Set in Garamond Monotype
Printed in England by Clays Ltd, St Ives plc

Contents

ALBERTO CAEIRO

RICARDO REIS

ÁLVARO DE CAMPOS

To
Linda Gutiérrez
Helder Macedo
David Pinner
Anthony Rudolf
Michael Schmidt
Judith Thurman

Introduction

Four Poets in One Man

Thus play I in one Prison, many people.

Fernando Pessoa is the extreme example of what may be the essentially modern kind of poet: the objective introvert. None has more consistently tried to find his real self with its multiplicity intact and to keep his poems impersonal. He accepted the dividedness of a human self so completely that he did something unique: wrote poetry under four names – his own and three 'heteronyms'. Not pseudonyms: they are imaginary poets with real poems in them. Fernando Pessoa was four poets in one: Alberto Caeiro, Ricardo Reis, Álvaro de Campos and himself; each strongly distinct from the others.

One is soon struck by an external difference between their poems. Those of Caeiro are in free verse; so (though very different in tone) are nearly all those of Campos; those of Reis metrical but unrhymed; Pessoa's own, except a few of the early ones, metrical and closely rhymed. This may have come about unconsciously, but was surely no accident. Pessoa was a poet who wrote poets as well as poems: he was two kinds of poet – dramatic, lyric. When he wrote as himself, he sang – in traditional metres, although the content of his songs is a modern mind caught at moments of self-confrontation, against a background of shadow. So he meets the present need for poetry that is both lyrical and searching, a poet who sings to our age. At the same time Pessoa was a dramatic poet who wrote poets instead of plays. One should enjoy the poems of the heteronyms as separate poems; but it is good sometimes to take them, instead, as lines or speeches in one of those three large-scale dramatic poems called *Poemas Completos de Alberto Caeiro, Odes de Ricardo Reis* and *Poesias de Álvaro de Campos*. One then sees that Pessoa was the pioneer of a new kind of long poem, which would in fact answer certain twentieth-century needs – an open-ended dramatic monologue. Besides being a singer on a par with Yeats, Pessoa created three of this century's viable long poems.

He was born in Lisbon on 13 June 1888, and died there on 30 November 1935. When still a small child he lost his father; his mother married again, and he was given an English education in Durban, where his step-father was the Portuguese consul. At seventeen he returned to Lisbon, and for thirty years – the rest of his life – he hardly stirred from there. Writing letters in English and French for commercial firms in Lisbon earned him a modest living and left him free to devote his life to poetry. He never married, and his love life was inhibited and sad. At times he was very active in Portuguese literary affairs, notably in 1915, when the avant-garde review *Orpheu* raised a storm and, though short-lived, made a lasting difference. He 'knew every-one' but had few close friends. One of these, the highly gifted poet Mário de Sá-Carneiro, committed suicide in Paris in 1916, at the age of twenty-six. Pessoa published very little in his life-time. He wrote most of his early poems in English (a sad waste – many fine things lost in poems that, like Eliot's French ones, do not really work), and of these he published two small books. Of his poems in Portuguese, a few appeared from time to time in little magazines; but the only book of them he published was *Mensagem* (Message) – forty-four patriotic poems which form, as he said, one poem.* In his last year, however, he more or less prepared for publication the works of the three heteronyms and a selection of his own poems, just over a hundred and fifty, to be called provisionally *Cancioneiro* (Song-book). When he died – of sudden hepatitis brought on by heavy drinking – he left also a trunk stuffed with manuscripts, which included close on three hundred more poems. This output has gradually won him recognition as the greatest Portuguese poet since Camões.

So the life of this rebel in clerk's clothing was what is commonly called uneventful. There should be a word like 'inventful' to describe his real life, that restless alternation of disorder and control out of which the poems came. A note written by him in English and dated 30.10.08 (when he was twenty) says:

> One of my mental complications – horrible
> beyond words – is a fear of insanity, which
> itself is insanity.

Another (perhaps of the same date) says:

> I suffer – on the very limit of madness, I
> swear it – as if I could do all and was
> unable to do it, by deficiency of will.

*John of Gaunt's speech having shown that patriotic verse can be poetry of a high order, Pessoa in *Mensagem* showed this to be still true. Most of its poems also go beyond patriotism: those in which King Sebastian figures are metaphors for the religious quest, and those about the ordeals of the seafarers dramatize the poet's inner perseverance.

Was he performing Hamlet for his own benefit? Or was he Hamlet? In a letter to Mario Beirão (1.2.13) he wrote:

> I have my soul in a state of ideative
> rapidity so intense that I need to turn
> my attention into a diary, and, even so,
> the pages I have to fill are so many that
> some get lost ... and others are
> illegible ... The ideas I lose cause me
> an infinite torture, they survive
> themselves in that torture, obscurely
> other.

And this, from 'Personal Notes' written in English, possibly in 1910, is even more disquieting:

> I am now in full possession of the
> fundamental laws of literary art.
> Shakespeare can no longer teach me to be
> subtle, nor Milton to be complete. My
> intellect has attained a pliancy and a
> reach that enable me to assume any emotion I
> desire and enter at will into any state of
> mind. For that which it is ever an anguish
> and an effort to strive for, completeness, no
> book at all can be an aid.

He lived surrounded by people he knew, writers and others, committing suicide or going mad. His struggle to keep sane showed, at first, mainly in theoretical writings. Their significance is that they are concerned with the future: Pessoa was working out the next thing to be done in poetry. He saw that subjectivism – the indulgent personal lyric – had to be condemned. Replaced with what? As he came up to maturity Pessoa, like Pound, made theories first, then exemplified them in poems. His preoccupation with theory made sure that he would be ready and lucid when the inspiration came.

It came copiously in 1914, when the three heteronyms arose. How this happened Pessoa himself has told, in his letter of 13 January 1935, to A. Casais Monteiro. Even in childhood, he had held long dialogues with imaginary individuals, whom he not only heard but saw and named. In about 1912 he tried to write some pagan poems: it was a failure, but there stayed with him 'a vague portrait' of their writer – 'without my knowing, Ricardo Reis had been born'. Rather less than two years later, as a joke to play on Sá-Carneiro, he was trying to invent a complicated kind of bucolic poet. Then:

> On the day when I finally desisted – it was the 8th of March, 1914 – I went over to a high desk and, taking a sheet of paper, began to write, standing, as I always write when I can. And I wrote thirty-odd poems straight off, in a kind of ecstasy whose nature I cannot define. It was the triumphal day of my life, and I shall never be able to have another like it. I started with a title – 'The Keeper of Sheep'. And what followed was the apparition of somebody in me, to whom I at once gave the name Alberto Caeiro. Forgive me the absurdity of the phrase: my master had appeared in me. This was the immediate sensation I had.

As soon as he had written the thirty-odd poems of Caeiro's,

> I immediately seized another sheet of paper and wrote, also straight off, the six poems that make up Fernando Pessoa's 'Chuva

Obliqua'. Immediately and completely . . .
It was the return of Fernando Pessoa Alberto
Caeiro to Fernando Pessoa himself alone. Or
better, it was the reaction of Fernando
Pessoa against his own non-existence as
Alberto Caeiro.

He soon went on – 'instinctively and subconsciously' –
to discover some disciples for Caeiro:

I jerked the latent Ricardo Reis out of his
false paganism, discovered his name, and
adjusted him to himself, because at this
stage I already *saw* him. And suddenly, in
a derivation opposed to that of Ricardo Reis,
there arose in me impetuously a new
individual. At one go, and on the typewriter,
without interruption or correction, there
arose the 'Triumphal Ode' of Álvaro de
Campos – the Ode along with this name and the
man along with the name he has.

He then created an imaginary *coterie*:

I fitted it all into moulds of reality. I
graded their influences, recognized their
friendships, heard, inside me, their
discussions and divergencies of criteria,
and in all this it seemed to me that I, the
creator of it all, was the least thing there.
It is as if it all happened independently of
me. And it is as if it still happens like
that . . .

A fact not mentioned in the letter: the first six poems
of Ricardo Reis bear the same date (6 June 1914),
which suggests, though it does not prove, that they
too came in one rush.

Pessoa's heteronyms coped with a problem which

14

afflicts everyone writing now. 'I must say that,' one thinks, 'and yet how, in this day and age, can I? It is me, but only part of me. A part, but still essential. It will be false if I write it as I.' Any honest writer now has at times to make so many qualifications that they either overload his art or inhibit it, unless a *persona* enables him to explore without hedging. Pessoa set himself free by hiving off three great swarms of his thoughts and feelings, and by setting them free to grow into valid long poems, each the total output of an imaginary poet. *Personae* so real liberate readers as well as their author. The Douanier Rousseau embodied the myth of the innocent painter, and so became the *persona* which a group of innovating painters, among them Picasso, needed. Alberto Caeiro embodies the innocent poet, for Pessoa and for the rest of us.

'My master had appeared in me' is the really illuminating phrase. Pessoa meant it. He writes elsewhere:

> ... Some act on men ... like fire, which burns out all the accidental in them and leaves them bare and real, their own and truthful, and those are the liberators. Caeiro is of that race. Caeiro has that force ... So, operating on Reis, who had not yet written anything, he brought to birth in him a form of his own and an aesthetic person. So, operating on myself, he set me free from shadows and tatters, gave my inspiration more inspiration and my soul more soul.

What in Caeiro could have this force? Pessoa imagined Campos writing a memoir of Caeiro, who had died, and saying in it: 'My master Caeiro was not a pagan:

he was paganism.' And in some notes written in English Pessoa says:

> Even in our age . . . Caeiro . . . does breathe absolute novelty . . . To a world plunged in various kinds of subjectivisms, he brings Absolute Nature back again . . . Far from seeing sermons in stones, he never even lets himself conceive a stone as being a sermon. The only sermon a stone contains for him is that it exists . . . Out of this sentiment, or rather, absence of sentiment, he makes poetry.

In the memoir Campos is also made to say:

> And I suddenly asked my master Caeiro, 'are you content with yourself?' And he answered: 'No: I am content.' It was like the voice of the earth, which is all and nothing.

I find a meaningful likeness between Alberto Caeiro and Francis Ponge. Monsieur Ponge said recently that each kind of animal proves its value simply by existing and being able to propagate, and that this, to him, is *le sacré*. The two do have much the same philosophy-religion: 'absolute objectivism', Pessoa calls it. But their ways of conveying it are quite different. Francis Ponge is concrete and specific; but Caeiro does not tell us what kind of tree or flower he is speaking of; he does not name, he rarely describes. And yet one of his poems ends with the line:

> And by the way, I was the only nature poet.

What achieves concreteness is Caeiro's teaching and – conveyed largely through it – the figure of the Master, teaching, painstakingly. In Wordsworth also there is a strange sparing of specific detail, and the reason could be that a really great nature poet has to be a sage, his essential business being not to describe, but to show nature as the open door to the meaning of life. The style of Caeiro is an unostentatious anti-poetry – this in 1914. His 'poems' are the talk of a master to disciples as he walks along a hillside and rounds up sheep. His teaching – according to some notes in the name of Ricardo Reis – did for a moment seem to Pessoa 'the one source of consolation' for those who feel like exiles in modern life. Such people need a shot of 'the ancient serenity and grandeur' to save them from dangerous despair. The writers of Antiquity had no experience of our predicament, so that to read them makes things worse, 'as if a child played near me, exasperating my adult illness by his too simple simplicity'. Caeiro's *Keeper of Sheep* has 'all the simplicity, all the grandeur the ancients had', all their 'possession of things', but, being written in reaction against modern conditions, it 'gives us now as balsam what in the others was merely coolness'. Perhaps it does. When Octavio Paz says that Caeiro is 'what no modern poet can be: a man reconciled with nature', I think he for once goes too far: Gary Snyder, for instance, makes a good bid to be a modern poet reconciled with nature. To the young men and women who want to get clean of the system and are seeking 'serenity and grandeur' in perhaps the Zen way, the teaching of Caeiro, which expressed their purpose more than half a century before, has something to say.

The weakness of Caeiro lies, as Octavio Paz says shrewdly, not in his ideas, which indeed are his strength, but in 'the unreality of the experience he says he embodies': he is an 'Adam on a farm in the Portuguese countryside'. Pessoa needed a capital city even when his life there seemed a banishment. For him Caeiro's simplicity in its turn proved, within three months, too simple. So Pessoa had to find a consolation for the failure of his consolation. And this, I think, was the main function of the output he created for Ricardo Reis. Caeiro is what Pessoa longed to be and could not: Reis is the nearest that Pessoa could come to being Caeiro. A disciple of Caeiro, Reis works paganism into an ethical doctrine, part epicurean, part stoic, yet conscious of, and kept clear of, a human environment conditioned by Christianity; a doctrine for people in the modern world to live by, so as to suffer as little as possible. This disciple is very different from his master: instead of the innocent poet, a highly sophisticated one; instead of the loping free verse, odes closely constructed with an air of ease in neo-classic metres. Many people find the work of Ricardo Reis much less fine and moving than the other heteronyms. I do not. He is not cold, he is cooling it. Granted, some of the outward features – those metres reminding one of Horace but less varied, those addresses to Lydia, Neaera or Chloe – can be off-putting. But these work as alienation techniques: by depersonalizing, they set Pessoa free to say things he feels too deeply to say without distancing; and the classical convention enables him to say trite things again because true. Add the expressive syntax and the constant choice of the modest exact word, and the products are often poems of grace and strength, where the joy of the making comes through clear and pure. Some render with sad, calm straightforwardness a part of paganism which has its maximum meaning today:

human dignity facing the shortness of life with no promise of anything beyond. And from some of them, suddenly, there emerges the authentic White Goddess presence. Yet the Reis vision of the Greek world excludes the Dionysiac elements, and quite a number of the Reis poems seem chill, merely perfect, like the typography of Bodoni in his last period.

But the repressed Dionysiac Pessoa did burst out: in modern dress, of course. The modern dress was Álvaro de Campos. Through Campos, Pessoa saved himself from settling down into Reis; it is as though Dionysus saved him from Apollo. The *Triumphal Ode* (1914) is Whitmanesque not only in its verse but in its 'yes' to the modern city. The next year's vast *Sea-faring Ode* is a passionately receptive voyage in the modern world. As sustained free structures, these are at least the equals of *Howl* and *Kaddish*, and I would say Campos has the bigger extrovert-introvert range. Campos is Whitman having a nightmare in which he wakes up to find he is Laforgue. He starts as an extrovert, ends as an introvert; starts determined 'to feel all every way there is', and ends up obsessed, asking if he is real. He does sometimes seem to be only there to sign any poem of Pessoa's own that has demanded to be done in free verse. The trouble with open-ended long poems which remain works in progress is that the poet – in this case Pessoa – changes, and the work, confused by fresh starts, becomes a rag-bag. Pound's *Cantos* come to mind. They remind us that the quality of the rags counts. Late Campos poems can be very fine.

As a poet in his own name, Fernando Pessoa matured fully almost as soon as his heteronym poets appeared. Caeiro the ideal; Reis the good second best; Campos doing Pessoa's travelling for him: but no escape from coming home to the real exploring. The essence of Pessoa was religion and scepticism. And Caeiro did give his soul more soul. On 19 January 1915, after much hesitation, Pessoa wrote a long letter to Armando Cortes Rodrigues, in which he speaks of himself as 'fundamentally a religious spirit' and of his

> constantly greater awareness of the terrible
> and religious mission which every man of
> genius receives from God with his genius.

By this light he has come to detest 'art merely for art's sake' and to see recent literary activities of his own as 'only beginnings of my sincerity'. This applies even to Intersectionism, the theory which the *Chuva Obliqua* poems had illustrated. It does not apply to Caeiro, Reis and Campos: his output in their names

> is written *dramatically*, but is sincere
> (in my grave sense of the word), just as
> what King Lear says is sincere, who is not
> Shakespeare but a creation of his ... Into
> each of them I have put a deep conception
> of life, different in all three, but in all
> of them gravely alert to the mysterious
> importance of existing.

And so, 'slowly but surely, in the divine inner obedience of an evolution whose ends are occult to me', he is raising his projects and ambitions 'constantly more to the height of those qualities I have received'. But this evolution was also taking him where the three heteronyms could not freely go, since they had to work out their conceptions along their own lines and to stay more or less in character. Pessoa had in him a 'deep conception of life' which he could not hive off into a

20

heteronym. There is a 'take this cup from me' tone in the letter he wrote to Sá-Carneiro on 6 December 1915:

> I am physically besieged ... The possibility that the truth may lie there, in Theosophy, *me hante*. You must not think I am on the path of madness ... This is a grave crisis in a mind that is luckily able to take such crises.

He asks Sá-Carneiro to

> consider how Theosophy is an ultra Christian system – in the sense that it contains the Christian principles elevated to a point where they melt into some kind of beyond-God – and think of how much in it is fundamentally incompatible with my essential paganism.

This is the first element in his crisis, the second being that Theosophy, 'because it admits all religions', is 'just like paganism, which admits all the gods into its pantheon'. So:

> Theosophy terrifies me by its mystery and occultist grandeur, repels me by its essential humanitarianism and proselytism ... attracts me through having so much in common with a 'transcendental paganism' (my name for the way of thinking which I had reached), repels me by having so much in common with Christianity, which I do not admit.

Pessoa was not a naïf: anything but. He was looking for a meaning, not ruling out any possibility and not liking what he thought he found. He believed as a man believes who wishes he did not:

> Why did you give what I asked, Holiness?
> I know the Truth, at last, of the real Being.
> Would it had pleased God I should know less!

But his scepticism practically never rested and was at times, apparently, the only thing he believed in: a point of honour, the one joy left. And, living 'in the great oscillation between believing and half denying', the same honour in him insisted on his subjecting each poem of his own, especially the ones most disturbingly felt, to the mind's impersonal control. He thought, as Eliot said, that 'the more perfect the artist, the more completely separate in him will be the man who suffers and the mind which creates'; indeed, several of his poems have this as their subject. In a letter to Francisco Costa he described Shakespeare as 'the most insincere of all the poets there have been', a provocative expression for what Keats called 'Negative Capability'. Pessoa was one of the most thorough possessors and pursuers of negative capability since Shakespeare, not only because he wrote the poems of imaginary poets but also in most of his own poems.

This shifting conflict – between the religion he chose and the one which seemingly chose him, and again between religion and scepticism, patriotism and scepticism, scepticism and love – is the basic content of Pessoa's own poetry, from maturity till death. On the leading edge of modernism as Campos, as Pessoa himself he made new the old set forms of song and sonnet. I have found, in the close reading which translating is, that the variety of his songs is much greater than it seems at first. Although the language is limpid and fresh, Pessoa's negative capability enables him to leave intact all the 'uncertainties, mysteries, doubts', all the ambivalences on which the whole truth of experience depends. And just because of his strict impersonal control, those poems which are surely personal – especially his highly original, sadly honest love poems – are intensely poignant. So, in poem after poem, the end-effect is a lucid mystery: in a closed form, an open content. In this, to my mind, Pessoa comes close to Dante (whom he seems to have disliked for his Christian proselytism). Like Dante, Pessoa was intellectual and passionate; he held together the strands of intricate, elusive thought, and sang like Schubert. He was an extraordinarily complex man who wrote simply.

JONATHAN GRIFFIN

A NOTE ON THE SECOND EDITION

Since the typescript of this book was accepted for publication I have translated many more poems by Pessoa. In 1973 Volume X of the *Obras Completas de Fernando Pessoa* (Ática, Lisbon) appeared under the title *Novas Poésias Inéditas*: one hundred poems discovered since those in Volumes VII and VIII were collected, and these also include some of his finest work. The present book has a new final section, to show more fully the range and depth of the poems written by Pessoa as himself. (Those taken from Volume X have, after their dates, the letters NPI.)

J.G.

Some of these translations have appeared in *The Journals of Pierre Menard, Workshop,* the Carcanet Press *Fernando Pessoa,* and *Modern Poetry in Translation.*

23

Books for Further Reading

Fernando Pessoa: *Obras Completas*, Ática, Lisbon; the poems in Portuguese in 10 volumes.

Fernando Pessoa: *Obra Poética*, Aguilar, Rio de Janeiro; the poems in Portuguese, English and French, in one volume (India paper); 3rd edition, 1969.

Fernando Pessoa: *Pàginas Íntimas e de Auto-Interpretacao*, edited and prefaced by Jacinto do Prado Coelho and Georg Rudolf Lind; Ática, Lisbon.

Fernando Pessoa: *Pàginas de Doutrina Estética*, edited and prefaced by Jorge de Sena; Ática, Lisbon.

Octavio Paz: *Cuadrivio*; Mortiz, Mexico; four essays, of which one, 'El Desconocido de Sí Mismo', is on Pessoa.

Michael Hamburger: *The Truth of Poetry*; Weidenfeld & Nicolson, London.

Jacinto do Prado Coelho: *Diversidade e Unidade em Fernando Pessoa*; Império, Lisbon, 1949.

Georg Rudolf Lind: *Teoria Poética de Fernando Pessoa*; Inova, Porto, 1970.

João Gaspar Simões: *Vida e Obra de Fernando Pessoa*; Livraria Bertrand, Lisbon, 1970.

Fernando Pessoa

Three Poems from
Mensagem (Message)

Magellan

In the valley, flaring, a fire.
A dance is shaking the entire
Earth. And disformed dismembered shadows
In the black clearings of the valley
Suddenly across the slopes show and,
Shifting, are lost in the dark's folds.

Whose is the dance interred in night?
They are the sons of the Earth, the Titans,
Dancing the death of the seaman who meant
To clasp the maternal body round –
Be, to clasp it, the first of men.
Buried on a far shore in the end.

They dance not knowing the dead man's
Daring soul is still in command,
At the helm a wrist with no body, to steer
The ships through the rest of the end of space:
That he can compass the entire
Earth – even absent – with his embrace.

He's raped Earth. They, unaware,
Dance on by themselves there.
And shadows – disformed and dismembered
Till they are lost at the horizons –
Up the slopes from the valley climb to
Mountain silence.

Portuguese Ocean

Salt-laden sea, how much of all your salt
Is tears of Portugal!
For us to cross you, how many sons have kept
Vigil in vain, and mothers wept!
Lived as old maids how many brides-to-be
Till death, that you might be ours, sea!

Was it worth while? It is worth while, all,
If the soul is not small.
Whoever means to sail beyond the Cape
Must double sorrow – no escape.
Peril and abyss has God to the sea given
And yet made it the mirror of heaven.

Dom Sebastião, King of Portugal

Mad, yes, mad, because I would have greatness
Such as Fate gives to none.
No tamping down in me my sureness;
Therefore, where the sand dwells, the worn
Part of me stopped, not the enduring one.

This my madness, accept it, those who can,
Dare whatever it needs.
What, without madness, is a man
More than a beast after feeding,
A corpse adjourned, the half-alive breeding?

As She Passes

When I am sitting at the window,
Through the panes, which the snow blurs,
I see the lovely image, hers, as
She passes . . . passes . . . passes by . . .

Over me grief has thrown its veil: –
Less a creature in this world
And one more angel in the sky.

When I am sitting at the window,
Through the panes, which the snow blurs,
I think I see the image, hers,
That's not now passing . . . not passing by . . .

(5.5.02)

Song

Is it sylphs or gnomes playing? ...
The groves of pines have, through them
Brushing, shadows and lightest
Breaths of musical rhythms.

They undulate like those
Around unknown roadsides
Or someone among trees
Who now shows and now hides.

Remote, uncertain form
Of what will never be mine ...
I hardly hear and almost
Weep. Weep, don't know why.

So tenuous a melody,
I hardly know if it's heard
Or if it's merely the twilight,
The pines and I being sad.

But it stops, just as a breeze
Forgets the form of its griefs,
And now the only music
Is that of the pine groves.

(25.9.14)

She's Singing – the Harvestwoman

She's singing – the harvestwoman. Poor,
Likes to think she is happy – could be:
Sings and scythes. And her voice, purely
A cheerful anonymous widowhood,

Lifts and falls like a bird's tone
Crossing the doorstep-clean air,
Takes the curves of her intricate tune
Smoothly, shapes them to the end clear.

Listen! it carries joy and sorrows,
There's farmland and chores in that voice of hers
And – she sings as though she'd more
Reasons for singing than life has.

Ah, sing, – sing without reasoning!
In me what feels has to be thinking.
Let your voice at a venture spring
And through my heart spill, rising, sinking!

Ah! if I could be you, being I!
Have the gaiety, yours, unconscious,
And consciousness as well! O sky!
O fields, orchards! O songs! Knowledge

Weighs one down, and so short one's life!
Enter me, right in! Constitute
My soul your shadow – make it so light!
And then, taking me with you, out!

(1914/15)

Suddenly a Hand

Suddenly a hand, part of some occult haunting,
Between the folds of the night and of my sleep
Shakes me, and I awake, and in the deep
Neglect of night discern no face or movement.

Yet an old terror I have, immanent
And unburied, as though from a king's siege
Descends, and affirms itself my liege
Without command, without threat, without taunting.

And I can fee! my life – how on a string
Of Unconscious abruptly tightening
I am, by some nocturnal hand, controlled.

I feel that I am no one, only a shade
Of a face I don't see, being in its shade,
And in nothing exist as the dark's cold.

(14.3.17)

Ah! The Anguish

Ah! the anguish, the abject rage, the despair
Of not laying myself bare
In a cry's tone, not bleeding my heart dry
In one last, austere cry!

I speak – the words I say are a sound only:
Suffer – am I.
Ah! to extract from music the secret, the tone
Of its cry!

Ah! the fury – grief crying out in vain
Since the cries just strain
And reach silence that returns from the air
In the night, nothing there!

(15.1.20)

Christmas

A God's born. Others die. Reality
Has neither come nor gone: a change of Error.
Now we have another Eternity,
And always the one passed away was better.

Blind, Science is working the useless ground.
Mad, Faith is living the dream of its cult.
A new God is a word – or the mere sound.
Don't seek and don't believe: all is occult.

(? 1922)

Gomes Leal

The dim planet, sinister, consecrates
Some. Its irreversible rings are
Misfortune, sorrow, loneliness. Staring
Into space   the weird moons,   eight.

This man, a poet, Apollo in his lap brought
And paid to Saturn. The hand of lead started
To rise toward his high, afflicted heart
And, raised, fastened on it – bleeding, worn out.

Those eight moons of mania – no good
As long as that triple girdle denotes
Loneliness, failure, amaritude!

Yet from the night without end a trail floats,
The traces of malignant beauty: it
Is the moon beyond God, algid, unknown.

(? 1924)

Dense Clouds Wall Up

Dense clouds wall up all
The base of the occident
In swaggering black purples.

With night all things recline.
The chill sky is transparent.
No crumbling of rain.

And I don't know, is it pain
Or delight I have from the absent
Rain and serene night?

But then, I know and have known
Nothing. My soul's the present
Shadow of a presence gone.

All my feelings are spoors.
Only my thought senses . . .
The night grows cold with stars.

(1.5.29)

To the Blind and the Deaf I Leave

To the blind and the deaf I leave
The soul with boundaries,
For I try to perceive
All every way there is.

From the height of being aware
I contemplate earth and sky –
Innocently I stare:
Nothing I see is mine.

But I see so alertly,
Disperse myself in them so
That each thought turns me
Diverse at a blow.

And just as things are splinters
Of being, and are dispersed,
I break the soul to slivers
And into different persons.

And if I see my own
Soul with a fresh gaze,
I ask if that offers any
Chance I should judge and seize.

Ah, as much as the land, sea or
Vast sky, a man
Who believes he is his is astray.
I'm various and not mine.

37

And so, if things are splinters
Of the knowledge of the universe,
Let me be my own slivers,
Imprecise and diverse.

If all I perceive is alien
And I am absent from me,
How came it the soul
Ends up in a body?

Therefore I harmonize
Myself with what God made:
A diverse mode God has,
I   am diverse modes.

God, therefore, I imitate –
Who, when He made all,
Removed from it   the infinite
And unity as well.

(24.8.30)

Sleep While I

Sleep while I keep watch . . .
Let me dream, give me leave . . .
Of joy smiling toward you
There's nothing in me. I want you
For dreaming, not for love.

Your calm flesh chills
The wanting in my seeing.
My desires are ache on ache
And I don't want to take
In my arms my dream of your being.

Sleep, sleep, sleep,
Vague there in your smiling . . .
I dream you so intently
The dream 's an ensorcelment
And I dream without feeling.

She Brings the Surprise of Being

She brings the surprise of being.
Is tall, a subdued gold.
Simply to think of seeing
Her half-mature body does good.

Her tall breasts would seem two
Hills (were she lying down)
Dawning without going through
Any twilight dawn.

The hand of her white arm settles,
Its span spread wide, to press
Lightly her side – the subtle
Swell of her form in the dress.

She's tempting like a boat.
Has something of bud and shoot.
God! when do I go aboard?
Hunger! when is it I eat?

(10.9.30)

Audible Smile of the Leaves

Audible smile of the leaves,
Just the wind at that place,
If I gaze at you and you gaze
At me, who is it that smiles
First? The first to smile laughs.

Laughs, and gazes suddenly
So as not to gaze,
At where can be sensed in leaves
The noise of the breeze as it goes.
All is breeze and disguise.

But the gaze has returned from long
Gazing where gaze there's none;
And we two stand talking on
Of what words, as usual, shun.
Is it ending or begun?

(27.11.30)

No: Don't Say a Thing

No: don't say a thing!
To suppose what your mouth,
Veiled there, will be saying
Is to be hearing it now –

Is to hear it, for certain,
Better than you would say it.
What you are doesn't come to the surface
Of sentences and days.

You are better than you.
Don't say anything: be!
Grace of the body nude –
Out of sight, and we see.

(5/6.2.31)

Harvestwoman

But no, she's abstract, is a bird
Of sound in the air of air soaring,
And her soul sings unencumbered
Because the song's what makes her sing.

(1932)

Rage in the Dark, the Wind

Rage in the dark, the wind –
Huge sound of on and on.
My thought has nothing in it
Except that it can't die down.

The soul contains, it seems,
A dark where there hardens and
Blows a madness that comes
From trying to understand.

Raving in dark, the wind –
It can't shake free out there.
My thought – I am caught in it
Like the wind caught in the air.

(23.5.32)

Why, O Holy One

Why, O Holy One, did you spill your word
Over my life?
Why does my false start have to have
This crown of thorns, the truth about the world?

Formerly I was wise and had no cares,
Listened, at day's end, to the homing cows,
And the farmland was solemn and primitive.
Now that I have become the truth's slave,
The gall of having it is all I have.
I am an exile here and, dead, still live.

Cursed be the day on which I asked for knowledge!
More cursed the one that gave it – for you did!
Where now is the unconsciousness – mine, early –
Which consciousness, like a suit, keeps hid?
I know, now, almost all and am left sighing . . .
Why did you give what I asked, Holiness?
I know the truth, at last, of the real Being.
Would it had pleased God I should know less!

(1932)

I Know, I Alone

I know, I alone
How much it hurts, this heart
With no faith nor law
Nor melody nor thought.

Only I, only I
And none of this can I say
Because feeling is like the sky –
Seen, nothing in it to see.

(10.8.32)

She Came Looking Elegant

She came looking elegant – speed
Without haste – with a smile too –
And I, who feel with the head,
Made – pat – the poem due.

In the poem I do not treat
Of her, girl adult, turning
The corner of that street
Which is the corner, eternal.

In the poem I treat of the sea,
Wave and grief are my matter.
Re-reading recalls for me
The hard corner – or the water.

(14.8.32)

Ah, All Is Symbols

Ah, all is symbols and analogies!
The wind on the move, the night that will freeze,
Are something other than night and a wind –
Shadows of life and of shiftings of mind.

Everything we see is something besides.
The vast tide, all that unease of tides,
Is the echo of the other tide – the sea
Alluned – there, where the world that is is real.

Everything we have 's oblivion.
The frigid night and the wind moving on –
These are shadows of hands, whose gestures are the
Illusion which is this illusion's mother.

(9.11.32 – *from notes for a Faust play*)

I See Boats Moving

I see boats moving on the sea.
 Their sails, like wings of what I see,
Bring me a vague inner desire to be
Who I was without knowing what it was.
So all recalls my home self and, because
It recalls that, what I am aches in me.

(1932)

Steps Linger

Steps linger in the grasses
Between moonlight and moonlight.
All is scent and woodland.
It feels as if someone passes.

Passes, treading lightly
Ground the moon has unsaid,
In a blanched gulp, the lightness
Of that light tread.

Is it elf, is it gnome, is it fairy,
The form no one perceives?
I remember: nothing was there.
I feel, and yearning believes.

(5.9.33)

I'm Scanning Things I Can't See

I'm scanning things I can't see.
It's late, near dark, and all
I yearn for within me
Stands checked before the wall.

The sky is huge above;
I can sense trees beyond;
Though hardly, now, any wind,
There are leaves on the move.

All's on the other side –
All there is, and my thought what it means.
And no bough being stirred
Can make the sky not immense.

What is merges with what
I sleep and am. And I'm
Not feeling; sad I'm not.
But a sad thing I am.

(7.9.33)

If I, Though Nobody

If I, though nobody,
Could have   on my face
That clearing light which those
Trees have fugitively,

I would have joy, the one
Which things get from outside.
But joy is the hour's, it
Departs with the cooled sun.

To me something had meant
More than the life I have –
To have the life from afar
Which just the sun had sent!

(16.9.33)

I Sleep. At Waking —

I sleep. At waking – if I dreamed, I do not
Know what my dream had in it.
I sleep – if without dreaming, I wake up
In front of a space, open,
Unfamiliar since what I woke to meet
Is what I don't know yet.
Best is to neither dream nor not dream and
Unwake without end.

(19.9.33)

Raining

Raining. There is silence, since rain's self
Makes no noise unless a noise of peace.
Raining. The sky's gone to sleep. When the soul is
Widowed of unknowing, feeling gropes.
Raining. My essence (who I am) I repeal.

So calm the rain is, it seems to disappear
(Not even made of clouds) into air, seems
Not to be rain even, only a whisper
Which itself, in the whispering, dislimns.
Raining. Nothing gleams.

No wind is hovering. There is no sky
That I can feel. It's raining, distant, indistinct,
Like something certain which may be a lie,
Like what does lie to us, some great thing desired.
Raining. In me nothing's stirred.

(2.10.33)

Great Mysteries Inhabit

Great mysteries inhabit
The threshold of my being,
On its sill hop and sit
Great sparrows that watch, avid,
My late crossing to seeing.

They are birds full of abyss,
Like the ones in dream. Dare
I sound and think what is?
My soul's cataclysm, this
Threshold – my soul now there.

Then I wake from the dream mystery
And rejoice in the light – till it grows
Into day and for me sad horror
Seeing the threshold is terror
And each step is a cross.

(2.10.33)

The Wind, High

The wind, high in its element,
Makes me lonelier – now I am not
Lamenting, it   has to lament.

Is an abstract, fathomless sound,
Comes from the world's elusive end.
Its meaning is to be profound.

Tells me the all has nothing in it,
That virtue's not a shield, and
How the best   is to be silent.

(27.12.33)

This

They say I pretend or lie
All I write. No such thing.
It simply is that I
Feel by imagining.
I don't use the heart-string.

All that I dream or lose,
That falls short or dies on me,
Is like a terrace which looks
On another thing beyond.
It's that thing leads me on.

And so I write in the middle
Of things not next one's feet,
Free from my own muddle,
Concerned for what is not.
Feel? Let the reader feel!

(?1933)

Loop-Hole

In my dark intervals
When in me no one is there
And all is mists and walls
That life offers anywhere,

If, quickly raising my eyes
From where in me I lie low,
I see the far horizon
With sunset and sunrise flowing

I revive, am, realize
And, even should the out
There I forget in be false,
I want or seek nothing else.
I surrender my heart to that.

(?1934)

In the Great Oscillation

In the great oscillation between
Believing and half denying
One's heart swings on and on
Loaded with null knowing;

And, estranged from the known
By not knowing the pith,
It grasps for a second only
That being aware is faith –

The faith which stars are aware of
Because it's the spider that clings
In the web all weave:
Is the life before things.

(5.5.34)

There Was a Moment

There was a moment
When you let
Settle on my sleeve
(More a movement
Of fatigue, I believe,
Than any thought)
Your hand. And drew it
Away. Did I
Feel it, or not?

Don't know. But remember
And still feel
A kind of memory,
Firm, corporeal,
At the place where you laid
The hand, which offered
Meaning – a kind of,
Uncomprehended –
But so softly . . .
All nothing, I know.
There are, though,
On a road of the kind
Life is, things – plenty –
Uncomprehended.

Do I know whether,
As I felt your hand
Settle into place
Upon my sleeve
And a little, a little,

In my heart,
There was not a new
Rhythm in space?

As though you,
Without meaning to,
Had touched me
Inside, to say
A kind of mystery,
Sudden, ethereal,
And not known
That it had been.

So the breeze
In the boughs says
Without knowing
An imprecise
Joyful thing.

(9.5.34)

Cease Your Song

Cease your song!
Cease, for along with
It I have heard
Another voice
Coming (it seemed) in
Interstices
Of the charm, softly strong,
Brought by your song as
Far as us.

Heard you and heard
It at the same
Time and distinct –
Two singing in time.
And that tune
– If now, unreal
As it was, I recall it –
Makes tears come.

Was your voice
Then an enchantment
Which, unwilling,
At that moment
Vaguely awoke
Some being (alien
It was to us,
And to us   spoke)?

Who knows? No, don't
Sing! Let me listen

What kind of silence
Will venture after
You   singing.

Ah, nothing, nothing!
Only the burdens
Of having heard,
Of having tried
To hear beyond
What sense a voice
Does carry in it.

At your raising
Your voice, what angel
– And you not knowing –
Swung low, grazing
(Almost) this earth
Where the soul ranges,
And fanned with his wings
Embers on an
Unknown hearth?

No more song! Must
Now have silence,
To sleep clear
Some remembrance
Of the voice heard,
Not understood,
Which was lost
For me to hear.

(9.5.34)

In This World

In this world, where we do oblivion,
We are shadows of who we are,
And the true gestures that we have in
The other which, being souls, we live in
Are startings and grimaces here.

Everything is nocturnal, clouded,
That there is, here among us:
Prolongations, finely divided
Smoke of the light which shines occluded
To such gazing as life allows.

But one or other of us, one moment,
Gazing properly, may perceive
In the shadow and its movement
What, in the other world, is meant
By that gesture which makes him live.

He comes face to face with the meaning
Of what's reduced, here, to grimacing,
And turns on his own body's journeying,
Understood from imagining,
The intuition of a gaze.

Longed-for shadow of the body,
Lie that answers to the lace
Tying it to the marvellous
Truth which casts it, eager, unsteady,
Upon the field of time and space.

(9.5.34)

In the Dead Afternoon's Gold More

In the dead afternoon's gold more –
The no-place gold dust of late day
Which is sauntering past my door
And will not stay –

In the silence, still touched with gold,
Of the woods' green ending, I see
The memory. You were fair of old
And are in me . . .

Though you're not there, your memory is
And, you not anyone, your look.
I shake as you come like a breeze
And I mourn some good . . .

I've lost you. Never had you. The hour
Soothes my anguish so as to leave,
In my remembering being, the power
To feel love,

Though loving be a thing to fear,
A delusory and vain haunting,
And the night of this vague desire
Have no morning.

It Begins to Be

It begins to be going to be dawn –
The black sky is beginning,
In a still-dark slight
Unblackening of its night,
To have a chill tint,
There, where the black is thinning.

A black that is azure-ashen
Outwards, vaguely, drifts
From where the Orient sleeps
Its late sleep, shapeless,
And a windless chill keeps station,
Heard, scarcely perceived.

And yet I, who have hardly
Slept, don't feel night or chill
Or, coming in, dawntide
From the void solitude.
The indefinite of the heart,
Its void, is all I feel.

In vain the day is dawning
To one who can't sleep, never
Was made to get things straight
Here inside the heart;
Who while he lives is denying
And, when he loves, does not have.

In vain, in vain, and the sky
Azures itself through green

Asheningly. What
Is it my soul feels? Not
That, no, nor even I,
In the night, which will soon be unseen.

(23.7.35)

Your Eyes Go Sad

Your eyes go sad. You're not
Listening to what I say.
They doze, dream, fade out.
Not listening. I talk away.

I tell what I've told, out of listless
Sadness, so often before . . .
I think you never listened,
So youraway you are.

All of a sudden, an absent
Stare, you look at me, still
Immeasurably distant,
You begin a smile.

I go on talking. You
Go on listening – your own
Thoughts you listen to,
The smile as good as gone,

Until, through the loafing
Afternoon's waste of while,
The silent self-unleafing
Of your useless smile.

(29.10.35)

There Are Diseases

There are diseases worse, yes, than diseases,
Aches that don't ache even in one's soul
And yet, that are more aching than the others.
There are dreamed anguishes that are more real
Than the ones life brings us, there are sensations
Felt only by imagining
Which are more ours than our own life is.
There's so often a thing which, not existing,
Does exist, exists lingeringly
And lingeringly is ours and us . . .
Above the cloudy green of the broad river
The white circumflexes of the gulls . . .
Above the soul the useless fluttering –
What never was, nor could be, and is everything.

Give me some more wine, because life is nothing.

(19.11.35)

At the Tomb of Christian Rosencreuz*

We had not yet seen the body of our prudent and wise Father.
For this we moved over to one side of the altar. Then we could
lift a strong plate of yellow metal, and there was a celebrated
fair body, entire and uncorrupted . . ., and he held in his hand a
little book of vellum, written in gold, entitled T., which is,
after the Bible, our highest treasure nor must be lightly
submitted to the censure of the world.

(*Fama Fraternitatis Roseae Crucis*)

1
When, awakened from this sleep, life, we know
Who we are, and what it was – this fall   right
Into Body, this descent to the Night
Which swathes the limbs and senses of our Soul, –

Shall we then see for ourselves the hidden whole
Truth of what is or flows? know it at sight?
No: that's not known even to the freed Sprite . . .
Not God, Who made us, has it in Him. No . . .

God is the Man of another God, greater:
Supreme Adam, He also had His Fall;
He also, just as He was our Creator,
Was created, and to Him the Truth died . . .
The Abyss, His Spirit, bans it Him from the far side;
Here, in the World His Body, there's none at all.

2
But in the beginning was the Word, occluded

*See Translator's Note at end of poem.

Here when the Infinite Light, now snuffed,
Was brought from Chaos, ground of Being, and fed
To the Shadow, and the absent Word was clouded.

Yet if the Soul perceives her own form blundered
In herself, which is Shadow, she at last sees, splendid,
The Word of this World, human and anointed,
Perfect Rose that in God is crucified.

Then we, lords of the threshold of the Skies,
Can go searching beyond God to surprise
The Master's Secret and the profound Good;

Not from here only, from us now, aroused,
Freed at last in the actual blood of Christ
From the World's generation – its death to God.

3
Ah, but here, where we blunder about, unreal,
We sleep who we are; and the truth – even say
We may at last in one of our dreams see all,
We see it, because dreaming, in a false way.

Shadows looking for bodies, if we reach one,
How then feel its, our, reality?
With hands of shadow, Shadows, what do we touch
    then?
Our touch is absence and vacuity.

Who is offering, from this locked soul, freedom, the
    open?
We don't see out, we hear beyond this hall –
Entity. But how comes, here, the door open?

Calm in his false death, to our gaze exposed
With, on his breast, the Book lying closed,
Our Father Rosaeacruz knows and is silent.

Translator's Note: The symbols and beliefs of the Rosicrucian order have inspired quite a number of artists, among them of course W. B. Yeats. There is no known mention before the *Fama Fraternitatis R.C.*, published in 1614, and its slightly later supplement, the *Confessio*. They tell us that Christian Rosencreuz was born in 1378, travelled in the Near East and Morocco, returned to Germany with secret wisdom, which he imparted to 3 – eventually 8 – disciples, and died at the age of 106. It was laid down that the order should remain secret for a hundred years. One hundred and twenty years after the founder's death, his hidden tomb was discovered by one of the then members. It contained the uncorrupted body and some precious documents and symbols. The members dispersed, having covered the vault over again, and no-one knows where it is. Pessoa's poem uses the myth with characteristic precision and openendedness. It is a drama – faith and doubt in swaying conflict – compressed into three stanzas, each a sonnet.

Alberto Caeiro

Poems from *The Keeper of Sheep*

I
I never kept sheep,
But it is as if I did watch over them.
My soul is like a shepherd,
Knows the wind and the sun,
And goes hand in hand with the Seasons
To follow and to listen.
All the peace of Nature without people
Comes to sit by my side.
But I remain sad like a sunset
As our imagining shows it,
When a chill falls at the far side of the valley
And you feel night has come in
Like a butterfly through a window.

But my sadness is calm
Because it is natural and right
And is what there should be in the soul
When it is thinking it exists
And the hands are picking flowers without noticing
    which.

At a jangle of sheep-bells
Beyond the bend of the road,
My thoughts are contented.
Only, I am sorry I know they are contented,
Because, if I did not know it,
Instead of being contented and sad,
They would be cheerful and contented.

To think is uncomfortable like walking in the rain
When the wind is rising and it looks like raining more.

I have no ambitions or wants.
To be a poet is no ambition of mine.
It is my way of staying alone.

And if I do want, sometimes,
For the sake of imagining, to be a lambkin
(Or to be the whole flock
So as to move spread out all over the hill-side,
Be many things happy at the same time),
It is only because I feel what I write at sunset,
Or when a cloud passes its hand over the light
And a silence flows across the open grass.

When I sit down to write verses,
Or, as I walk along the roads or short cuts,
Write verses on the paper that is in my thought,
I feel a shepherd's crook in my hands
And see an outline of myself
There on the hill-crest,
Listening for my flock and seeing my ideas,
Or listening for my ideas and seeing my flock,
And smiling vaguely like a man who does not
    understand what is being said
And tries to pretend he understands.

I salute all those who may read me,
Doffing my broad-brimmed hat to them
As they see me in my doorway
And the bus barely makes it to the hill-crest.
I salute them and I wish them sun,
And rain, when rain is needed,

And that their houses may have
Just below an open window
A favourite chair
Where they may sit, reading my verses.
And, as they read my verses, may they think
I am some natural thing –
For instance, the ancient tree
In whose shade, when children,
They sat down suddenly, tired of playing,
And wiped the sweat from the hot forehead
With the sleeve of the striped smock.

5
There is ample metaphysics in not thinking at all.

What do I   think about the world?
How should I know what I think about the world?
If I were ill I would think about it.

What idea have I about things?
What opinion do I have on causes and effects?
What meditations have I had upon God and the soul
And upon the creation of the World?
I don't know. For me, to think about that is to shut
    my eyes
And not think. It is to draw the curtains
Of my window (but it has no curtains).

The mystery of things? How should I know what
    mystery is?
The only mystery is there being somebody who might
    think about mystery.
A man who stands in the sun and shuts his eyes
Begins not to know what the sun is
And to think many things full of heat.

But he opens his eyes and sees the sun,
And now he cannot think of anything,
Because the light of the sun is worth more than the
    thoughts
Of all the philosophers and all the poets.
The light of the sun does not know what it is doing
And so does not stray and is common and good.

Metaphysics? What metaphysics do those trees have?
That of being green and having crowns and branches
And that of giving fruit at their hour, – which is not
    what makes us think,
Us, who don't know how to be aware of them.
But what better metaphysics than theirs,
Which is not knowing why they live
And not knowing they don't know?

'Inner constitution of things' . . .
'Inner meaning of the Universe' . . .
That is all false, it all means nothing.
It is incredible that people can think about those things.
It is like thinking of reasons and ends
When the beginning of the morning is there with
    rays, and over the edges of the trees
A misty lustrous gold   sweeps, dispersing the
    darkness.

To think about the inner meaning of things
Is waste of effort, like thinking about health
Or taking a glass to the water of the fountains.

The only inner meaning of things
Is their having no sort of inner meaning.

I don't believe in God, because I never saw him.
If he wanted me to believe in him,
He would certainly come and talk with me,
Would come in through my doorway
Saying to me, *Here I am!*

(Perhaps that sounds ridiculous to the ears
Of one who doesn't know what it is to look at things,
Doesn't understand a man who talks of them
In the way of talking which the sight of them teaches.)

But if God is the flowers and the trees
And the hills and the sun and the moonlight,
Then I believe in him,
Then I believe in him at every hour,
And my life is all a prayer and a mass,
And a communion with the eyes and through the ears.

But if God is the trees and the flowers
And the hills and the moonlight and the sun,
Why do I call him God?
I call him flowers and trees and hills and sun and
    moonlight;
Because if, for me to see him, he makes himself
Sun and moonlight and flowers and trees and hills,
If he appears to me as being trees and hills
And moonlight and sun and flowers,
It is that he wants me to know him
As trees and hills and flowers and moonlight and sun.

And therefore I obey him
(What more do I know of God than God of Himself?),
I obey him by living, spontaneously,
Like one who opens his eyes and sees,

And I call him moonlight and sun and flowers and
    trees and hills,
And I love him without thinking of him
And think of him by seeing and hearing,
And I walk with him at every hour.

7
From my village I see as much as from earth one can
    see of the Universe . . .
Therefore my village is as big as any other earth
Because I am the size of what I see
And not the size of my own height . . .

In the cities life is smaller
Than here at my home upon the crest of this hill.
In the city the houses shut the view and lock it,
Hide the horizon, push our gaze far away from all the
    sky,
Make us small because they take away from us what
    our eyes can give us,
And make us poor because our only wealth is to see.

13
Lightly, lightly, very lightly
A wind, a very light one, passes
And goes away, still very lightly.
And I don't know what I think
And have no wish to know.

14
I don't bother with rhymes. It is seldom
That there are two trees equal, side by side.
I think and write as the flowers have colour
But with less perfection in my way of expressing myself

Because I lack the divine simplicity
Of being all only my outside.

I look and am moved,
I am moved as water flows when the ground is sloping,
And my poetry is natural like the rising of a wind . . .

24
What we see of things are the things.
Why should we see one thing if there were another
    there?
Why should to see and hear be to delude ourselves
If seeing and hearing are seeing and hearing?

The essential is to be good at seeing,
Good at seeing without always thinking,
Able to see when one is seeing,
And not think when one is seeing
Nor see when one is thinking.

But that (poor us who carry our soul fully clothed!),
That demands a thorough course of study,
An apprenticeship in unlearning
And a sequestration into the liberty of that convent
Of which the poets say that the stars are the eternal
    nuns
And the flowers the passionate penitents of one sole
    day,
But where in the end the stars are nothing but stars
And the flowers nothing but flowers,
This being why we call them stars and flowers.

25

The soap-bubbles this child
Keeps blowing from a reed
Are translucently a whole philosophy.
Bright, purposeless and transient like Nature,
Friends of the eyes like things,
They are what they are
With a rounded and aerial precision,
And no one, not even the child who is letting them
    loose,
Pretends that they are more than what they seem.

Some are scarcely seen in the light-filled air.
They're like the breeze, which passes and barely
    touches the flowers
And which we know is passing
Only because something gets air-borne in us
And accepts everything more lucidly.

26

At times, on days of flawless and exact light,
When things have all the reality they can have,
I stop and ask myself
Why even I attribute
Beauty to things.

Has a flower somehow beauty?
Is there beauty somehow in a fruit?
No: they have colour and form
And existence only.
Beauty is the name of something that does not exist
Which I give to things in exchange for the pleasure
    they give me.

It signifies nothing.
And yet why do I say of things: they are beautiful?

Yes, even I, who live only by living,
Am caught up invisibly in the lies of men
About things,
About things which simply exist.

How difficult to be just oneself and not see anything
    but the visible!

30
Should they want me to have a mysticism, right, I have
    one.
I'm mystical, but only with the body.
My soul is simple and does not think.

My mysticism is not to try to know.
It is to live and not think about it.

I don't know what Nature is: I sing her.
I live on the crest of a hill
In a whitewashed house that stands apart,
And this is my definition.

44
I wake up in the night suddenly
And my watch is occupying the whole of night.
I can't feel Nature there outside.
My room is a dark thing with walls vaguely white.
Out there, there is a calm as though nothing existed.
Only the watch continues its clatter.
And that little object of cog-wheels there on my table
    top

Smothers the whole existence of the earth and of the
   sky . . .
I almost lose myself in thinking what it may signify,
But I stop short, and feel myself smiling in the night
   with the corners of my mouth,
Since the only thing my watch symbolizes or signifies
As it fills with its littleness the enormous night
Is the curious sensation of filling the enormous night
With its littleness . . .

47
One wildly clear day,
The kind when you wish you had done a pile of work
Not to have to do any that day,
I caught sight, like a road ahead among trees,
Of what may be the Great Secret,
That Great Mystery the false poets speak of.

I saw that there is no Nature,
That Nature does not exist,
That there are mountains, valleys, plains,
That there are trees, flowers, grasses,
That there are streams and stones,
But that there's not a whole to which this belongs,
That any real and true connection
Is a disease of our ideas.
Nature is parts without a whole.
This perhaps is that mystery they speak of.

This was what without thought or even a pause
I realized must be the truth
Which all set out to find and do not find
And I alone, because I did not try to find it, found.

49

I take myself indoors and shut the window.
They bring the lamp and give me goodnight,
And my contented voice gives them goodnight.
O that my life may always be this:
The day full of sun, or soft with rain,
Or stormy as if the world were coming to an end,
The evening soft and the groups of people passing
Watched with interest from the window,
The last friendly look given to the calm of the trees,
And then, the window shut, the lamp lit,
Not reading anything, nor thinking of anything, nor
    sleeping,
To feel life flowing over me like a stream over its bed,
And out there a great silence like a god asleep.

from *The Shepherd in Love*

High in the sky, there goes the Spring moon.
I think of you and inside me stand complete.
Here comes, through the broad meadows, running to
    me, a light breeze.
I think of you, murmur your name; and am not me:
    am happy.
Tomorrow you'll come, you'll walk with me to pick
    flowers in the meadow.
And I shall walk with you through the meadows to see
    you picking flowers.
I see you now tomorrow picking flowers with me in
    the meadows,
Because, when you come tomorrow and walk with me
    through the meadow, picking flowers,
That will be a lightness and a truth for me.

(6.7.14)

The Water Gurgles

The water gurgles in the mug I raise to my mouth...
'It's a cool sound' says to me someone who's not
    drinking it.
I smile. The sound is only of gurgling.
I drink the water and hear nothing with my throat.

(29.5.18)

If, After I Die

If, after I die, they should want to write my biography,
There's nothing simpler.
I've just two dates – of my birth, and of my death.
In between the one thing and the other all the days are
    mine.

I am easy to describe.
I lived like mad.
I loved things without any sentimentality.
I never had a desire I could not fulfil, because
    I never went blind.
Even hearing was to me never more than an
    accompaniment of seeing.
I understood that things are real and all different from
    each other;
I understood it with the eyes, never with thinking.
To understand it with thinking would be to find them
    all equal.

One day I felt sleepy like a child.
I closed my eyes and slept.
And by the way, I was the only Nature poet.

Ricardo Reis

Master, Serene

Master, serene are
All hours
We waste, if in
The wasting them,
As in a jar,
We set flowers.

There are no sorrows
Nor joys either
In our life.
So let us learn,
Thoughtlessly wise,
Not to live it,

But to flow down it,
Tranquil, serene,
Letting children
Be our teachers
And our eyes be
Filled with Nature.

On the stream's edge,
On the road-verge,
It falls right –
In always the same
Light respite
From being alive.

Time passes,
Tells us nothing.

We grow old.
Let's learn, as though
Tongue in cheek,
To watch us going.

It's not worth while
To make a gesture.
There's no resisting
The cruel god
Who devours forever
His own sons.

Let us pick flowers,
Let's dip lightly
These hands of ours
In the calm streams,
That we may learn
Calm like them.

Sunflowers ever
Eyeing the sun,
From life let's go
Tranquilly, not have
Even the remorse
Of having lived.

(12.6.14)

Crown Me with Roses

Crown me with roses,
Crown me really
    With roses –
Roses which burn out
On a forehead burning
    So soon out!
Crown me with roses
And with fleeting leafage.
    That will do.

(12.6.14)

Apollo's Chariot Has Rolled

Apollo's chariot has rolled onwards
Out of sight. The dust it raised
Has stayed behind, filling with subtle
    Mist the horizon.

That calm flute – it is Pan's – launching
Its clear-cut tones on the idle air
Has added sadnesses to the gracious
    Day that is dying.

Warm and golden, nubile and sad
Girl, weeder on the parched farmland,
You stay on, listening (your feet
    More and more dragging)

To the ancient flute of the god persisting
With the air a subtle breeze is swelling,
And I know you are thinking of the clear goddess
    Born of the seas,

And waves are moving there, far in,
In what your tired body is feeling
While still the flute, smiling, is weeping,
    Pallidly mourning.

(12.6.14)

The Roses of the Gardens of Adonis

The roses of the gardens of Adonis
Are what I love, Lydia, those flitting roses
   That in the day when they are born,
     Within that day, die.

The light's for them eternal, because they
Are born with the sun born already, and sink
   Before Apollo may yet leave
     The visible course he has.

Like them, let us make of our lives *one day*, –
Voluntarily, Lydia, unknowing
   That there is night before and after
     The little that we last.

(11.7.14)

The Gods Do Not Consent

The gods do not consent to more than life.
Let us refuse everything that might hoist us
    To breathless everlasting
    Pinnacles without flowers.
Let's simply have the science of accepting
And, as long as the blood beats in our fountains
    And the same love between us
    Does not shrivel, continue
Like window-panes, transparent to the lights
And letting the sad rain trickle down freely,
    At the hot sun just lukewarm,
    And reflecting a little.

(17.7.14)

The Ancient Rhythm

The ancient rhythm which belongs to bare feet,
That rhythm of the nymphs, pattern repeated,
    When in the grove's shade
    They beat out the dance sound,
Remember, you, and do it, on the white
Shore which the sea-foam leaves dark; you, still
   children
    Who are not yet cured
    Of being cured, restore
Rousingly the round, while Apollo bends,
Like a high branch, the blue curve which he goldens,
    And the perennial tide
    Runs on, flowing or ebbing.

(9.8.14)

Hate You, Christ, I Do Not

Hate you, Christ, I do not, or seek. I believe
In you as in the other gods, your elders.
    I count you as neither more nor less
    Than they are, merely newer.

I do hate, yes, and calmly abhor people
Who seek you above the other gods, your equals.
    I seek you where you are, not higher
    Than them, not lower, yourself merely.

Sad god, needed perhaps because there was
None like you: one more in the Pantheon, nothing
    More, not purer: because the whole
    Was complete with gods, except you.

Take care, exclusive idolater of Christ: life
Is multiple, all days different from each other,
    And only as multiple shall we
    Be with reality and alone.

(9.10.16)

Solemn over Fertile Country

Solemn over fertile country passes
The white cloud, ineffectual, fugitive,
Which from among the fields for one black instant
Raises a lukewarm breath.

Flying high in my soul the slow idea
Blackens my mind, but already I am turning
– Like the field's self to itself – to the daylight
Of imperfect life.

(31.5.27)

In Broad Daylight Even the Sounds

In broad daylight even the sounds shine.
On the repose of the wide field they linger.
    It rustles, the breeze silent.
I have wanted, like sounds, to live by things
And not be theirs, a winged consequence
    Carrying the real far.

The Wind at Peace

The wind at peace
Is creeping softly over deserted fields.
It is as if
What is . . . grass trembles with a tremor of
Its own, rather than the wind's.
And though the mild and high clouds are
Moving, it is as if
The earth were whirling fast and they were passing,
Because of great height, slowly.
Here in this wide quiet
I could forget all –
Even the life I disrecall
Would have no lodge in what I recognize.
Their false course my days would in this way
Savour true and real.

(27.2.32)

I Stick to Facts

I stick to facts. Just what I feel, I think.
Words   are ideas.
Rustling, the stream passes – and what does not pass,
Which is ours, not the stream's.
I'd have had verse be like that: mine is alien,
Something that I too read.

(16.6.32)

To Be Great, Be Entire

To be great, be entire: of what's yours nothing
    Exaggerate or exclude.
Be whole in each thing. Put all that you are
    Into the least you do.
Like that   on each place   the whole moon
    Shines, for she lives aloft.

(14.2.33)

I Want

I want – unknown, and calm
Because unknown, and my own
Because calm – to fill my days
With wanting no more than them.

Those whom wealth touches – their skin
Itches with the gold rash.
Those whom fame breathes upon –
Their life tarnishes.

To those for whom happiness is
Their sun, night comes round.
But to one who hopes for nothing
All that comes is grateful.

(2.3.33)

Legion Live in Us

Legion live in us;
I think or feel and don't know
Who it is thinking, feeling.
I am merely the place
Where thinking or feeling is.

I have more souls than one.
There are more 'I's than myself.
And still I exist
Indifferent to all.
I silence them: I speak.

The crisscross thrusts
Of what I feel or don't feel
Dispute in the I I am.
Unknown. They dictate nothing
To the I I know. I write.

(13.11.35)

Álvaro de Campos

Excerpts from *Triumphal Ode*

Ah, to be able to express myself whole as a motor
    expresses itself!
To be complete like a machine!
To be able to go through life triumphal like an
    automobile, the very latest model!
Be able at least to permeate myself physically with all
    that,
Rip myself right open, lay myself bare completely,
    render myself passive
To all the oil and heat and carbon perfumes
Of that stupendous, black, artificial and insatiable
    flora!

Hi, streets! Hi, squares! Heyhiho *la foule*!
Every passer-by, every window-shopper!
Dealers; vagrants; exaggeratedly well-dressed conmen;
Obvious members of exclusive clubs;
Down-at-heel dubious figures; vaguely contented
    family men
Paternal even to the gold watch-chain which spans the
    waistcoat
From pocket to pocket!
Every passer-by, all that passes and never passes!
Over-emphasized presence of the tarts;
Interesting banality (and who knows what it is like
    inside?)
Of the well-to-do ladies, mother and daughter usually,
Moving along the street with some purpose or other;
The feminine, false grace of homosexuals, passing by,
    slowly;

And all the simply elegant people who stroll and let
    themselves be seen
And have after all each a soul in there!

(Ah, how I would love to be the pimp of all that!)

Tobacconist's

I am nothing.
Never shall be anything.
Cannot will to be anything.
This apart, I have in me all the dreams of the world.

Windows of my room,
Room of one of the millions in the world about whom
    nobody knows who he is
(And if they knew who he is, what would they know?),
You give on the mystery of a street constantly
    trodden by people,
On a street inaccessible to all thoughts,
Real, impossibly real, certain, strangely certain,
With the mystery of the things under the stones and
    lives,
With death to put damp in the walls and white hair
    on men,
With Destiny to drive the car of all down the
    roadway of nothing.

I, today, am defeated, as though I knew the truth.
I, today, am lucid, as though I were just going to die
And had no longer any connection with things
Except a leave-taking, this house and this side of the
    street turning into
The line of carriages of a train, and a whistle blown
    for departure
From inside my head,
And a jolt to my nerves and a creaking of bones at
    moving off.

III

I, today, am perplexed, like a man who has thought
    and found and forgotten.
I, today, am divided between the loyalty I owe
To the Tobacconist's on the other side of the street,
    as a thing real outside,
And to the sensation that all is dream, as a thing real
    inside.

I have failed altogether.
As I have not achieved any design, perhaps it was all
    nothing.
The apprenticeship they gave me –
I've dropped from it out of the window at the back of
    the house.
I went out into the country with grand designs.
But there I met with only grass and trees,
And when there were people they were just like the rest.
I move from the window, sit down in a chair. What shall
    I think about?

What do I know of what I shall be, I who don't know
    what I am?
Be whatever I think? But I think so many things!
And there are so many people thinking of being the
    same thing of which there cannot be all that many!
Genius? At this moment
A hundred thousand brains are busy dreaming of
    themselves as geniuses like me,
And history will not mark – who knows? – even one,
And nothing but manure will be left of so many future
    conquests.
No, I don't believe in me . . .
All the lunatic asylums have in them patients with
    many many certainties!

And I, who have no certainty at all, am I more certain
    or less certain?
No, not even in me . . .
In how many garrets, and non-garrets, in the world
Are there not at this hour geniuses-in-their-own-eyes
    dreaming?
How many high and noble and lucid aspirations –
Yes, really and truly high and noble and lucid –
And who knows whether realizable? –
Will never see the light of the real sun, or reach the
    ears of people?
The world is for the person who is born to conquer it,
And not for the one who dreams he can conquer it,
    even if he be right.
I have dreamed more than Napoleon performed.
I have squeezed into a hypothetical breast more
    lovingkindnesses than Christ,
I have made philosophies in secret that no Kant wrote.

But I am, and perhaps always shall be, the man of the
    garret,
Even though I don't live there;
I shall always be the *one who was not born for that*;
I shall always be the one who *had qualities*;
I shall always be the one who waited for them to open
    to him the door at the foot of a wall without a door,
And sang the ballad of the Infinite in a hen-coop,
And heard the voice of God in a well with a lid.
Believe in myself? No, and in nothing.
Let Nature pour out over my ardent head
Her sunshine, her rain, the wind that touches my hair,
And the rest that may come if it will, or have to come,
    or may not.
Heart-diseased slaves of the stars,

We conquer the whole world before getting out of bed;
But we wake up and it is opaque,
We get up and it is alien,
We go out of the house and it is the entire earth
Plus the solar system and the Milky Way and the
    Indefinite.

(Have some chocolates, little girl;
Have some chocolates!
Look, there's no metaphysics in the world except
    chocolates.
Look, all the religions teach no more than the
    confectioner's.
Eat, dirty little girl, eat!
If I could eat chocolates with the same truth as you do!
But I think and, peeling the silver paper with its fronds
    of tin,
I leave it all lying on the floor, just as I have left life.)

But at least there remains, from the bitterness of what
    will never be,
The rapid calligraphy of these verses –
Colonnade started towards the Impossible.
But at least I dedicate to myself a contempt without
    tears,
Noble at least in the big gesture with which I throw
The dirty laundry I am – no list – into the course of
    things
And stay at home without a shirt.

(You, who console, who don't exist and therefore
    console,
Either Greek goddess, conceived as a statue that might
    be alive,

Or Roman matron, impossibly noble and wicked,
Or troubadours' princess, most gentle and bright
    vision,
Or eighteenth-century marquise, décolletée and
    distant,
Or celebrated cocotte of one's father's time,
Or something modern – I've no very clear idea what –,
Be any of this whatever, and, if it can inspire, let it!
My heart is an overturned bucket.
Like the people who invoke spirits invoke spirits I
    invoke
Myself and meet with nothing.
I go to the window and see the street with absolute
    clarity:
I see the shops, I see the pavements, I see the traffic
    passing,
I see the living creatures in clothes, their paths crossing,
I see the dogs also existing,
And all this weighs on me like a sentence to
    banishment,
And all this is foreign, as all is.)

I have lived, have studied, have loved, and even
    believed,
And today there is not a beggar I do not envy simply
    for not being me.
I look at each one's rags and ulcers and lying,
And I think: perhaps you never lived or studied or
    loved or believed
(Because it is possible to do the reality of all that
    without doing any of it);
Perhaps you have barely existed, like when a lizard's
    tail is cut off
And it is a tail short of its lizard squirmingly.

I have made of me what I had not the skill for,
And what I could make of me I did not make.
The fancy dress I put on was the wrong one.
They knew me at once for who I was not and I did not
    expose the lie, and lost myself.
When I tried to take off the mask,
It was stuck to my face.
When I got it off and looked at myself in the glass,
I had already grown old.
I was drunk, was trying in vain to get into the
    costume I had not taken off.
I left the mask and went to sleep in the cloakroom
Like a dog that is tolerated by the management
Because he is harmless
And here I am, on the point of writing this story to
    prove I am sublime.

Musical essence of my useless verses,
If only I could meet with you as something of my own
    doing,
Instead of staying always facing the Tobacconist's
    opposite,
Trampling underfoot consciousness of existing,
Like a carpet that a drunk stumbles over
Or a doormat the gipsies stole and was worth nothing.

But the Lord of the Tobacco Store has come to the
    door and stopped in the doorway.
I look at him with the unease of a head twisted askew
And the unease of a soul understanding askew.
He will die and I shall die.
He will leave the shop-sign, I shall leave verses.
At a certain stage the shop-sign also will die, and the
    verses also.

After a certain stage the street where the shop-sign
    was will die,
And the language the verses were written in.
Later will die the revolving planet on which all this
    took place.
On other satellites of other systems something like
    people
Will continue making things like verses and living
    under things like shop-signs,
Always one thing opposite another,
Always one thing as useless as another,
Always the impossible as stupid as the real,
Always the underlying mystery as sure as the sleep
    of the surface mystery,
Always this or always some other thing or neither one
    thing nor the other.

But a man has gone into the Tobacconist's (to buy
    some tobacco?)
And plausible reality has descended suddenly over me.
I half rise energetic, convinced, human,
And resolve to write these verses in which I say the
    contrary.

I light a cigarette as I think of writing them
And I savour in the cigarette liberation from all
    thought.
I follow the smoke like a route of my own
And enjoy, for a sensitive and competent moment,
Liberation from all speculations
And awareness that metaphysics is a consequence of
    feeling out of sorts.

Then I sink into my chair

117

And continue smoking.
As long as Destiny concedes it, I shall continue
     smoking.

(If I married the daughter of my laundress
Perhaps I would be happy.)
At this I get up from the chair. I go to the window.

The man has come out of the Tobacconist's (putting
     change into his trousers pocket?).
Ah, I know him; it's Steve, he has no metaphysics.
(The Lord of the Tobacco Store has come to the door.)
As if by some divine instinct Steve has turned and has
     seen me.
He has waved me a greeting, I have shouted to him
     Adeus ó Estêves, and the universe
Has rebuilt me itself without ideal or hope, and the
     Lord of the Tobacconist's has smiled.

(15.1.28)

In the Terrible Night

In the terrible night, natural substance of all nights,
In the night of insomnia, natural substance of all my
    nights,
I remember, awake in tossing drowsiness,
I remember what I've done and what I might have
    done in life.
I remember, and an anguish
Spreads all through me like a physical chill or a fear,
The irreparable of my past – this is the real corpse.
All the other corpses may very well be illusion.
All the dead may be alive somewhere else,
All my own past moments may be existing somewhere
In the illusion of space and time,
In the falsity of elapsing.

But what I was not, what I did not do, what I did not
    even dream;
What only now I see I ought to have done,
What only now I clearly see I ought to have been –
This is what is dead beyond all the Gods,
This – and it was, after all, the best of me – is what not
    even the Gods bring to life . . .

If at a certain point
I had turned to the left instead of to the right;
If at a certain moment
I had said yes instead of no, or no instead of yes;
If in a certain conversation
I had hit on the phrases which only now, in this
    half-sleep, I elaborate –
If all this had been so,

I would be different today, and perhaps the whole universe
Would be insensibly brought to be different as well.

But I did not turn in the direction which is irreparably lost,
Not turn or even think of turning, and only now I perceive it;
But I did not say no or say yes, and only now see what I didn't say;
But the phrases I failed to say surge up in me at present, all of them,
Clear, inevitable, natural,
The conversation gathered in conclusively,
The whole matter resolved . . .
But only now what never was, nor indeed shall be, hurts.

What I have missed definitely holds no sort of hope
In any sort of metaphysical system.
Maybe I could bring what I have dreamed to some other world,
But could I bring to another world the things I forgot to dream?
These, yes, the dreams going begging, are the real corpse.
I bury it in my heart for ever, for all time, for all universes,

In this night when I can't sleep and peace encircles me
Like a truth which I've no share in,
And the moonlight outside, like a hope I do not have, is invisible to me.

(11.5.28)

De La Musique

Ah, little by little, between the ancient trees,
Her figure emerges and I cease to think . . .

Little by little, from the anguish of me, I myself begin
    emerging . . .

The two figures meet in the clearing by the
    lakeside . . .

. . . The two dream figures,
Because this was only a ray of moonlight and a sadness
    of mine,
And a supposition of something different,
And the result of existing . . .

Did, really and truly, the two figures meet
In the clearing by the lakeside?
                (. . . But if they don't exist? . . .)

. . . In the clearing by the lakeside? . . .

(17.9.29)

I Have a Terrible Cold

I have a terrible cold,
And everyone knows how terrible colds
Alter the whole system of the universe,
Set us against life,
And make even metaphysics sneeze.
I have wasted the whole day blowing my nose.
My head is aching vaguely.
Sad condition for a minor poet!
Today I am really and truly a minor poet.
What I was in the old days was a wish; it's gone.

Goodbye for ever, queen of the fairies!
Your wings were made of sun, and I am walking here.
I shan't get well unless I go and lie down on my bed.
I never was well except lying down on the Universe.

Excusez un peu . . . What a terrible cold! . . . it's
    physical!
I need truth and the aspirin.

(14.3.31)

In the House Opposite

In the house opposite me and my dreams
What happiness there always is!

Strangers to me live there, people I have seen but
    not seen.
They are happy because I don't know.

The children who play on the high balconies
Live between vases of flowers,
Without a doubt, eternally.

The voices that rise from within that home
Are always singing, without any doubt.
Yes, they must be singing.

When it is a holiday here outside, it's a holiday there
    within.
It has to be like that where everything fits –
Man into Nature, because the town is Nature.

What a great happiness not to be me!

But may not the others feel that way too?
What others? There are no others.
What the others feel is a house with the window closed,
Or, when it opens,
It is to let the children play on the railed terrace,
Between the vases of flowers – I never saw what kind.

The others never feel.

The one who feels is us,
Yes, all of us,
Even I who at this moment am feeling nothing.

Nothing? I don't know . . .
A nothing which hurts . . . .

(16.6.34)

At Times I Have

At times I have happy ideas,
Ideas suddenly happy, in among ideas
And the words in which they naturally shake free . . .

After writing, I read . . .
What made me write that?
Where have I been to find that?
Where did that come to me from? It is better than
  me . . .
Shall we have been, in this world, at the most, pen
  and ink
With which somebody writes properly what we here
  jot? . . .

(18.12.34)

Newton's Binomial Theory

Newton's binomial theory is as beautiful as the Venus
   of Milo.
The fact is, precious few people care.

OIOIOIOI---OIOIOIOIOIOIOI OIOIOI---
   OIOIOIOIOIOIOI   OIOIOIOIOIOIOIOIOI

(The wind out there.)

The Ancients Used to Invoke

The ancients used to invoke the Muses.
We invoke ourselves.
I don't know if the Muses appeared –
Invoked and invocation must have had some
   conformity –
But I know we don't appear.
How often I have leaned
Over the well I suppose I am
And bleated 'Ah!' to hear an echo,
And have not heard more than what I saw –
The vague dim dawn-grey of the water answering the
   light
Down there in the uselessness at the bottom . . .
No echo for me . . .
Only, vaguely, a face,
Which must be mine since it can't be someone else's.
It is a thing almost invisible,
Except as and when luminously I see
There at the bottom . . .
In the silence and the false light at the bottom . . .

What a Muse! . . .

(3.1.35)

I Am Tired

I am tired, that is clear,
Because, at a certain stage, people have to be tired.
Of what I am tired, I don't know:
It would not serve me at all to know
Since the tiredness stays just the same.
The wound hurts as it hurts
And not in function of the cause that produced it.
Yes, I am tired,
And ever so slightly smiling
At the tiredness being only this –
In the body a wish for sleep,
In the soul a desire for not thinking
And, to crown all, a luminous transparency
Of the retrospective understanding . . .
And the one luxury of not now having hopes?
I am intelligent: that's all.
I have seen much and understood much of what I
    have seen,
And there is a certain pleasure even in the tiredness
    this brings us,
That in the end the head does still serve for
    something.
(24.6.35)

Pessoa as Pessoa

Poems added 1982

Vision

There is a country, measureless – but real
More than the life the world appears to have,
And more than Nature itself natural
To the frightening truth of being alive.

Under a sky that's single – placid – normal
Where (it appears) not a thing stirs or is,
Where neither a wind moans nor, inexorable,
The idea of a cloud   sets to work, grows,

It lies – a land? no – there is no   soil
But, foreign, freezing, despair to the soul
Who sees that country there, without veil, lie

Rigidly in the infinites of room
Silent, a forest of discarnate arms
Unprofitably raised towards the sky.

(5.3.10)

The Madman

And talks to constellated skies
Past the bars and past his hurts
Perhaps with dreams that are like mine . . .
Perhaps with, my God, what true words!

The bars of a constricting cell
Separate him from sky and land . . .
Puts human hands to the bars, and yells
In a voice not of human kind . . .

(30.10.28)

We Took the Town
After an Intense Bombardment

The child with the golden hair
Lies on the crown of the road.
Has his guts outside
And, by its bit of cord,
A train, and is unaware.

His face is now a mish-
mash of blood and nothing.
There glitters a small fish
– The kind for a bath-tub –
Over by the kerb.

Dark swathes the street featureless.
One gleam still, far-off, gilds
The upbringing of the future . . .

And   the golden child's?

(n. d., published in O *Notícias Ilustrado* 14.1.29)

Your Voice Keeps Talking Lovingly

Your voice keeps talking lovingly . . .
Speaks so sweetly that I've forgotten
Its mild chatter's falsity.
My heart is ready to unsadden.

Music suggests things that are not
There in the music: so – yes, true –
My heart asks nothing more than that
Melody which there is in you.

Love me? Who thought it, ever? Speak
On in that voice saying nothing – haply
You   are a delusive music.
I listen, don't know, and am happy.

And there's no happiness that is false;
It is true while it will stay.
Who cares what the truth exalts
If I am happy in this way?

(22.1.29)

In the Huge Hours

In the huge hours when insomnia is looming
As though a new sorrowful universe,
And the mind's clear like a man's figure condemning
The confused use that makes day otiose,

I reflect, plunged in shadows of repose
Where ghosts dwell and the soul is cased in gloom,
How much I've erred – how sorrow or carouse,
Either, like a crass phrase, will do nothing to me.

I reflect, full of nil, and night is all.
My heart, which talks as it stays mute, still
Repeats its one-note torpor without feature

In shadow, in lucidity delirium,
And there's no God, no self, even no Nature.
One's own heartbreak had been a better sorrow.

(31.8.29, NPI)

Past the Window There

Past the window there
Whose curtain never stirs
I place the vision of her
Whom the soul in itself construes
From desire revealing her fair.

I am not short of love,
Do not lack being wanted.
But another taste it would have
If it were elsewhere, if
In back of that tall window.

Why? – If I knew, I'd have won
All that I long for. Of old
I was in love with the Queen,
And since then there has been
In my soul a throne to be filled.

And still I set in there the
Throne, provided I
May dream still and see nothing:
Beyond the curtain's the hearth,
Beyond the window the dream.

So I go on relieving
The journey and the labour
With a little self-oblivion
For I now ask nothing of living
Except to be her neighbour.

(25.12.30)

I Don't Own Any Farm

I don't own any farm.
If I want one for dreaming about,
I have to extract it from
The mist of my soft thought.

And then, unmaking the fog
There always is in us,
Up, bit by bit, I drag it
And a farm on its own there it is.

I see the ponds, see the chutes
Water is trickling down,
See the tracks with their ruts,
The threshing-floor, bare, serene.

Contented with this nothing
Which in myself I flesh,
I enjoy the grassland freshness
Of the unfarm I go to earth in.

Holiday, unreachable,
To us for recall I bequeath it –
And forget it home to the original
Level of my soft thought.

(30.3.31, NPI)

I Still Keep

I still keep, like an amazement
In which childhood's not dead,
Half the enthusiasm –
Have it because I did.

Almost at times feel shame,
So much I believe what I don't.
It is a kind of dream
With reality right in it.

Sunflower of false delight
Around the centre's silence –
Yellow, amazed, utters
The black centre that's all.

(18.4.31)

Guides Me? Reason, Lonely

Guides me? Reason, lonely –
No more's been given to guide me.
Does it light me vainly?
It alone does light me.

Had He Who made the world
Desired I should be other
Than I am, He would
Himself have made me other.

He gave me eyes to see.
I look, see, trust.
How should I dare to say
'Blind, I had been blest'?

Like looking, God gave me
Reason, to make me see
Out   beyond vision –
Looking of cognition.

If to see's to deceive me,
To think a going astray,
Don't know – God chose to give me
Them for truth and way.

(23.5.32)

Death's the Road-Bend

Death's the road-bend, to die
's to be out of sight, no more.
I hear, real as I,
You going on before.

Earth is made of heaven.
Lies have nests? Not they.
No-one's been lost, ever.
All is truth and way.

(23.5.32)

When Nothing is Left Us

When nothing is left us, then is
When the mute sun
Is good.   The forest silence
Is many sounds without sound.

The breeze smiles enough.
Afternoon is someone forgetting.
Vagueness strikes the leafage
And more than the branch is unsteady.

To have had hope is eloquent
Like a story told as a song.
When the forest falls silent
The forest speaks on.

(9.8.32)

The Ancient Censer

The ancient censer, among rifts
And ornamental gold, swings high.
Absorbed without attention, I
Follow the slow steps of the ritual.

But the arms are invisible
And those chants are chants which are not
And the censer belongs to other levels
Which are seen and heard by the heart.

Ah, faultlessly the ritual chooses
Its rhythms and its steps always –
The not there ritual arouses;
A soul's what it is, not has.

The censer is in sight, swinging.
There, in the air, heard, is the chant.
But the ritual at which I am present
Is a ritual of remembering.

In the great Temple before birth,
Before   life and soul and God . . .
And the floor of the ritual, its chessboard,
Is what today is the heavens and earth.

(22.9.32)

I Listen Without Looking

I listen without looking and so see
Through the grove nymphs and fauns stepping a
   maze
Between trees that cast shade or dread, beneath
Branches which whisper as they feel my gaze.

But who   was it, did pass? No-one knows that.
I rouse up   and hear   the heart beat –
That heart which has in it no room for what
Is left after illusion has leaked out.

Who am I, I who am not my own heart?

(24.9.32)

When, With Some Reason Or

When, with some reason or
None, on the soul's wide fear
The shadow of death comes,
The spirit is seeing clear
– A clearness without calm –
How life passing is shadow,
How life ceasing is sorrow,
And loves life more.

(10.2.33, NPI)

The Laundress at the Pool

The laundress at the pool
Pounds clothes upon stone truly.
Sings because sings, is grieving
Because sings because living;
Therefore is cheerful too.

If only I could ever
Succeed in doing with verses
What she does to the clothes,
Maybe I might lose
My destinies, their diverseness.

There's a great unity
In – without any thought,
And half singing, maybe –
Pounding clothes really . . .
Who launders me my heart?

(15.9.33, NPI)

There Go, in the Army Stream

There go, in the army stream,
The soldiers – quick march
With the band playing them
The step they must keep, each.

I go in the life stream
With   a mystery band
Playing me how I'm bound
To stay in that lost march.

I go and sleep my rambling
Like the miller slumbering
Alone to the mill's rumbling.
I sleep, but feel I march.

(19.9.33, NPI)

If, By Chance, Estranged

If, by chance, estranged even from what I've dreamed,
I meet me in this world – alone, sans fellow –
And, true to what I myself disesteemed,
Treat as real my false footsteps, and follow,

There wakes in me – counter to the hope I saw
In this sort of escape, or simply haven –
No adjusting to the external law,
But taking that law as punishment given.

Then,   actually through   hope lifting
Me free from this   world of shapes and shifting,
I touch – through grief and faith – tentatively

Some other world, in which dream and life are
Null in a nothing, equal in the   dark,
And at all's end the Sunrise of what is.

(28.9.33, NPI)

I Dream – Fathomless

I dream – fathomless, endless.
I sleep – useless and issueless.
God sleeps – the world this is.

But if I also could
Sleep a sleep like God's
I   might dream the Good –

The Good of the Ill I exist.
That dream, I glimpse in the distance,
In me I call Christ.

Now, with His being absent,
Up looms what there is of present,
Eternally, in absence.

Not on the cross lifted
Above some calvary of life
But on a cross being lived

Has He been crucified
Who was pierced deep and wide
By a spear in His side.

And out from that heart
Of His, water and blood
Will come, but the truth not . . .

Only when, once descended
From where He was erected
To be despised and rejected,

His body shall next stoop
Before the place of the tomb,
Then shall I meet Him.

As long as the world has held,
In the world the soul has ailed
From what it destroys of the world.

As long as life may endure,
Life is bitterly sure
Of being mortal, impure.

And so   to the Cross
Life took, to have us
Viewed by the best of us.

The tomb which was shut tight
Was found, in morning light,
Open and cleared out.

My heart, too, is the grave
Of the Good, which to live
Is to want and not have.

But at my side there is
An angel, sees me and says
That all is otherness.

(2.7.34)

To Me Now Death's Coming

To me now death's coming is no such weight.
I now know it is nothing, fiction, dream,
And on the universal wheel of Fate
I am not what I here suppose I am.

I know there are more worlds than this not-much one
On which to us there does seem to be dying –
The harsh and craggy ground that is there, lying
Under the depth of living's immense ocean.

I know death, which is everything, is nothing,
And that, from death to death, the real soul
Does not fall in the well: moves on a path.
In His time and at ours God will say.

(6.7.34)

Your Profile, Your Gazing

Your profile, your gazing – real? a pose? –
Reminds me of that eternal moment when
I loved Semiramis, being the chosen
Of that calm vision then.

I loved her, clearly, without space or time
Having anything to do with that love.
Therefore from this thin love I protect my
Greater love, still alive.

But as I gaze at you, I remember it –
In who I am, who I have been sounds on
Already, when I loved Semiramis,
It was late in Fate, and the love soon gone.

How many lost voices have sung a part
In the lost centuries now come to be
An unreal memory in a heart!
How many 'live voices of nobody!

(21.7.34)

Ah, It Is

Ah, it is, it is the goddess! –
She whom none ever saw without
Loving, and whom the heart engoddesses
By divining her, simply that.

At last magnanimous she's coming
In   that perfectness whose truth
Is a statue which life is warming
And   makes   life itself faith.

Ah, it is, it is – close to her
In the gravemound world the dead
Man is dreaming, like the star
Which will   rise in the heaven depth.

(3.9.34)

Should Somebody One Day

Should somebody one day knock at your door
Announcing he's an emissary of mine,
Never believe him, nor that it is I;
For to knock does not go with my vainglory,
Even at the unreal door of the sky.

But should you, naturally and without hearing
Anyone knock, come to your door, unbar it
And find somebody waiting (it appears)
To dare to knock, give it some thought. It was
My emissary and I and the retinue of my glorying
In what drives to despair and what despairs.
Unbar to who does not knock at your door!

(5.9.34, NPI)

I Know I'm a Sick Man

I know I'm a sick man. I know
That in me who I am is missing.
Yes, but, as long as I'm not submitting,
I'd like to know the way I'm going.

Though I go towards submitting me
To the thing Destiny makes me be,
I *would* like, one moment, to stop
Here   and at my ease take stock.

There's great lapses of memory,
Great parallel lost lines
And a lot of legend and a lot of history
And lots of lives, lots of lives –

All that; from me now I am losing
Me, astray's where I go – I'd call
Out to me, and am enclosing
My self within recalling all.

I'd like, if it's mad I'm going to be,
To be mad sagely and morally.
I'm going, like Nero, to strum the lyre.
Only there's no need for the fire.

(15.9.34, NPI)

Soon as There are Roses

Soon as there are   roses, I want no roses.
I want them only when there can't be any.
    What should I do with the things, many,
    On which, at will, any hand closes?

I never want the night except when dawn
Is making it melt into gold and azure.
    That of which my soul is unsure
    Is what I must possess, that only.

For what? . . . If I knew that, I would not form
Verses to say I don't, even now, know it.
    I have a soul that's poor and cold . . .
    Ah, with what alms   shall I warm her? . . .

(7.1.35, NPI)

Advice

Ring with high walls the who you dream yourself.
After that, where the garden's visible
Through the wrought iron gate's affable grille,
Plant   all the most smiling kinds of flowers,
That only so may people know you at all.
Where no-one's going to see it, plant nil.

Fix flower-beds like those the neighbours have,
In which anyone peering may make out
Your garden as you mean them to descry it.
But where you're yours, and nobody sees ever,
Let such flowers as come from the soil sprout,
Leave the natural herbs free to run riot.

Fix a living double of you, guard it
And make sure no-one who comes there and gazes
Can know more than a garden of who you be –
A showy, at the same time private, garden
Behind which   the native flower grazes,
The herb so poor that even you don't see.

(n.d., first published in *Sudoeste*, no. 3, November 1935)

Love is the Essential

Love is the essential.
Sex, mere accident.
Can be equal
Or different.
A man's not an animal:
Is a flesh intelligent,
Although sometimes ill.

(5.4.35)

Azure, or Green, or Purple

Azure, or green, or purple when the sun
Goldens it with a false wash of vermilion,
The sea forbids, or idles, or leads on,
Is at times the abyss, at others mirror.
I summon up, as age moves in,
That in me which would want more than the sea
Now that nothing's there for discovery.

The great sea-captains and the crews with whom
They did the navigation of solitude
Lie far away, their reward in their gloom
Is our forgetting, our ingratitude.
Only the sea, when in storm mood
The waves are great and it is truly sea,
Seems remembering them uncertainly.

But I am dreaming . . . Sea is water, mere
Nude water, slave to the force, darkly felt,
Which, like poetry, comes from the moon
And at times will let fall, at others lift.
And yet, whatever descants float
Above the natural ignorance of the sea,
I still forefeel its murmur, oozily.

Who knows what the soul is? Who can make out
What soul there is in things which appear dead –
How much, in earth or nothing, can't forget?
Who knows whether space, the empty, is doored?
O dream, who thrust on me this duty
To meditate so on the voice of the sea,
How meditate on you? Teach that to me.

Captains, quartermasters – all argonauts
Of every day's landfall on unbelief –
Perhaps you heard, calling you, unknown flutes,
Their tune, elusive, unattainable.
Did your hearing perhaps follow
A being of the sea yet not the sea –
Sirens of hearing, not of victory?

One who beyond oceans without end
Has called you out towards the distance, or
One who knows there is, in our hearts of men,
Desire for good, natural, yet also more
Elusive, subtle – to the core
A thing which demands the sound of the sea,
And not to stop – far from all things still be.

If it is so, if the vast sea and you
Are something (you because you perceive, and
The sea by being) of this which I think true;
If, in existence's unknown profound,
There's more soul than can reach the vain
Surface of us, as though that of the sea, –
Make me, to unknow it, in the end, free.

Give me a soul transposed, an argonaut's,
And make me have, as the old sea-captain had,
Or his quartermaster, ears for the flute's
Call out of the distance to our heart, –
Make me hear' like a pardon, part
Remembrance of a teaching sunk in me,
The ancient Portuguese speech of the sea.

(9.6.35)